THIRD GRADE BOOK:
Science is Fun

SPEEDY PUBLISHING LLC

Speedy Publishing LLC
40 E. Main St. #1156
Newark, DE 19711
www.speedypublishing.com

Copyright 2015

ISBN: 978-1-6814-5466-5

First Printed 03/09/2015

Contents

Matter

Animals

Lesson I
Sea Animals

Octopus

A sea animal with eight tentacles, two eyes. It is a mollusk and an invertebrate, which means it has no bones in the body. There are more than 150 types of octopus.

The Dolphin

Dolphins are small members of the whale order, Cetacea. Dolphins are mammals and are noted for their intelligence and learning abilities.

Starfish

Sea stars or commonly known as starfish are marine animals that have a central body with rays. Starfishes are not fishes since they do not have backbones and are called invertebrate.

Turtles

Sea turtles are the turtles that live in the world's oceans. There are seven species, and they are split into two families: the Dermochelyidae and the Cheloniidae.

Crabs

Crabs are short-tailed crustaceans that may live either on land or in the sea. Many species, including the blue (Callinectes sapidus), Dungeness (Cancer magister), and king (Paralithodes camtschatica) crabs, are eaten buy humans.

Elephant Seals

Elephant seals are the largest members of the group of aquatic, fin-footed mammals called pinnipeds.

Fish

The word fish is often used to describe many animals that live in water. Worldwide nearly 1,200 species of fish have been identified as threatened with extinction.

Sea Horse

Nothing more unlike a fish could be imagined that the sea horse. In fact it looks much like the knight in a chess game. The sea horse has a head of and neck shaped like a horse, and it swims in an upright position.

Do you know other Sea Animals?

Desert Animals

Camel

The two species of large hoofed animals known as camels were domesticated about 4,000 to 5,000 years ago. Ever since, they have provided meat, milk, wool, and hides to various desert- and mountain-dwelling peoples of the Eastern and Western Hemispheres.

Snakes

Of all the animals, snakes are among the best known but perhaps the most misunderstood. Snakes are characterized by their elongated limbless bodies.

Fennec

A small pale fox with large pointed ears, native to the deserts of North Africa and Arabia.

Do you know other Desert Animals?

Forest Animals

Bear

Bears are large, powerful mammals related to dogs and raccoons. The biggest bears are the world's largest animals that live on land and eat meat.

Fox

Foxes are mammals that look like small, bushy-tailed dogs. They live all over the world. Different kinds favor different habitats.

Wild Boar

Wild boar is a specie of wild pig, native to the forests of Europe, north-west of Africa and also found throughout Asia.

Wolf

Believed to be an ancestor of the domestic dog, the wolf is a highly intelligent and courageous hunter. Its remarkable powers of endurance are legendary.

Squirrels

A small animal with a long tail and soft fur that lives in trees. They usually eat nuts.

Woodpecker

When a woodpecker drums a tree, it is usually looking for a food. Once it has detected the sounds of insects gnawing or moving withing the wood, it begins to hammer persistently in pursuit of its prey.

Hedgehog

When the spiny hedgehog is frightened or attacked, it rolls itself into a ball to protect its vulnerable face and underparts, exposing only its sharp prickly spines.

Deer

Members of the deer family are found throughout the Western Hemisphere, Europe and Asia.

Do you know other Forest Animals?

SECTION ACTIVITY

Identify if the animal is a sea, desert or forest animal.

1. Snake ___________________________

2. Fish ___________________________

3. Wild Boar ___________________________

4. Deer ___________________________

5. Woodpecker ___________________________

6. Starfish ___________________________

7. Camel ___________________________

8. Dolphin ______________________

9. Squirrels ______________________

10. Fennec ______________________

11. Hedgehog ______________________

12. Fox ______________________

13. Bear ______________________

14. Octopus ______________________

15. Crabs ______________________

Planets

Mercury
Venus
Earth
Mars
Jupiter
Saturn
Uranus
Neptune
Pluto

Mercury

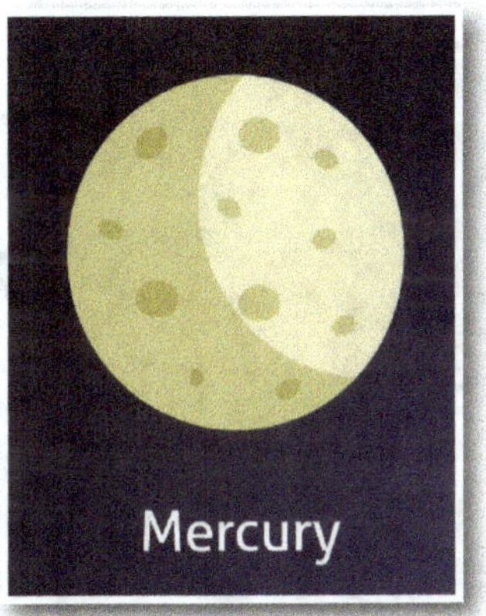

Mercury is the closest planet to the Sun and due to its proximity it is not easily seen except during twilight.

A year in Mercury is just 88 days long.

Mercury is the most cratered planet in the Solar System.

Venus

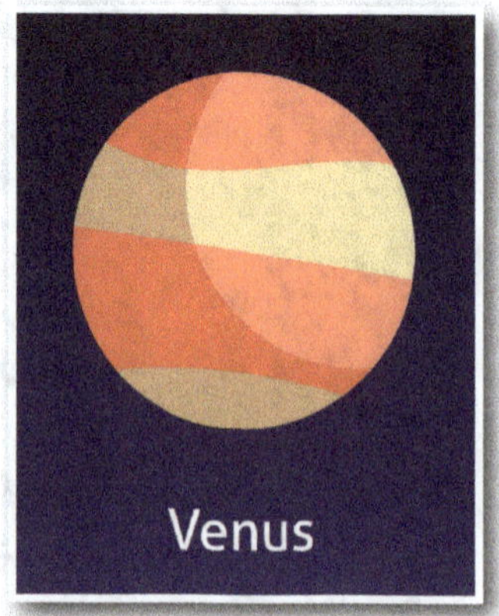

Venus is the second planet from the Sun and is the brightest object in the night sky after the Moon.

A day on Venus lasts longer than a year.

Venus rotates counter-clockwise.

Earth

Earth is the third planet from the Sun and the largest of the terrestrial planets.

The Earth has the greatest density.

It is where we live!

Mars

Mars is the fourth planet from the Sun. Named after the Roman god of war.

Mars is home to the tallest mountain in the solar system, the Olympus Mons.

Jupiter

The planet Jupiter is the fifth planet out from the Sun, and is two and half times more massive than all other planets.

Jupiter has the shortest day of all the planets—9 hours and 55 minutes.

Lesson 6

Saturn

Saturn is the sixth planet from the sun and the most distant that can be seen with the naked eye.

Saturn is the flattest planet

Saturn has the most extensive rings in the solar system.

Uranus

Uranus is the seventh planet from the Sun. It's not visible to the naked eye, and became the first planet discovered with the use of a telescope.

Uranus turns on its axis once every 17 hours and 14 minutes.

Neptune

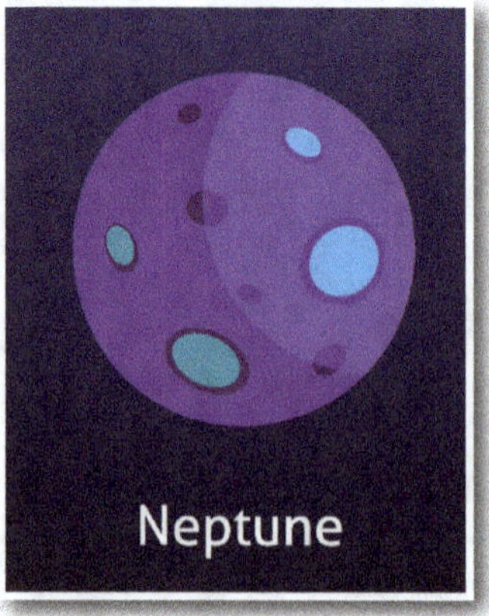

Neptune is the eighth planet from the Sun and is the most distant planet from the Sun.

Neptune has a very active climate.

It has 14 moons.

Pluto

The no longer major planet since 2006, Pluto is now considered a dwarf planet instead.

Pluto has 5 moons.

No spacecraft have visited Pluto.

SECTION ACTIVITY

Arrange the planets from the 1st closest to the moon to the most distant.

1. ________________   5. ________________

2. ________________   6. ________________

3. ________________   7. ________________

4. ________________   8. ________________

Earth	Venus
Neptune	Mercury
Uranus	Saturn
Mars	Jupiter

Matter

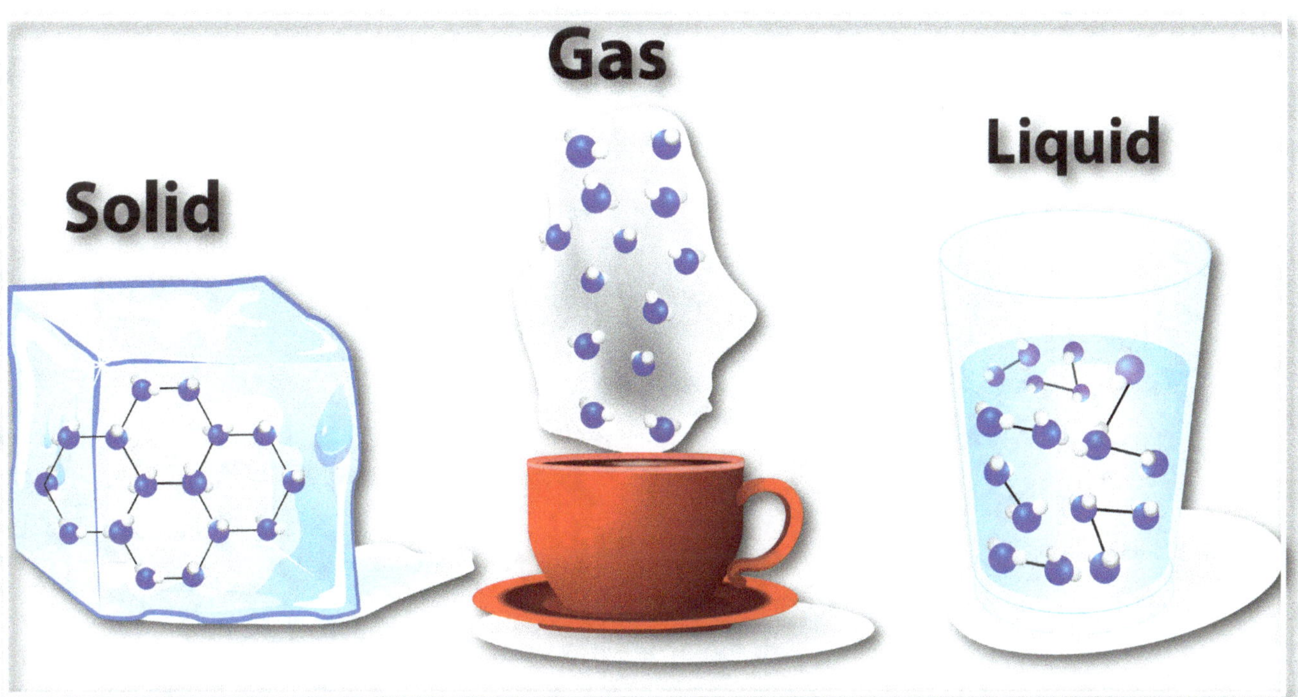

Lesson 1
Solid

A substance that retains its shape and shape without a container; a substance whose molecules cannot move freely except to vibrate.

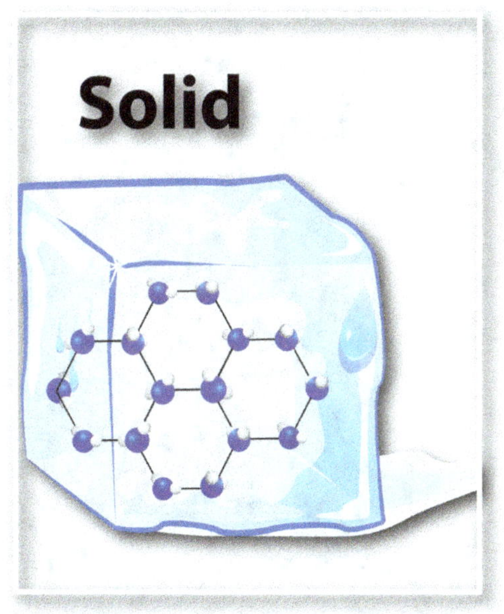

Liquid

A substance that flows and keeps no definite shape because its molecules are loosely packed and constantly moving. It takes the shape of its container but maintains constant volume.

Lesson 3

Gas

A substance that can only be contained if it's fully surrounded by a container (or held together by gravitational pull); a substance whose molecules have few intermolecular bonds and can move freely.

SECTION ACTIVITY

Identify if the object is a solid, liquid or gas.

1. Desk _______________

2. Milk _______________

3. Floor _______________

4. Block _______________

5. Air _______________

6. Oxygen _______________

7. Coffee _______________

8.   Tea   ______________________

9.   Carbon Dioxide   ______________________

10. Wood   ______________________

11. Tree   ______________________

12. Soda   ______________________

13. Chair   ______________________

14. Table   ______________________

15. Hydrogen   ______________________

SECTION ACTIVITY

Look at your surroundings. List down at least 3 solids and 3 liquids you see.

Solid

1.

2.

3.

Liquid

1.

2.

3.

NOTES

NOTES

Answers

Identify if the animal is a sea, desert or forest animal.

1.	Snake	**Desert Animal**
2.	Fish	**Sea Animal**
3.	Wild Boar	**Forest Animal**
4.	Deer	**Forest Animal**
5.	Woodpecker	**Forest Animal**
6.	Starfish	**Sea Animal**
7.	Camel	**Desert Animal**
8.	Dolphin	**Sea Animal**
9.	Squirrels	**Forest Animal**
10.	Fennec	**Desert Animal**
11.	Hedgehog	**Forest Animal**
12.	Fox	**Forest Animal**
13.	Bear	**Forest Animal**
14.	Octopus	**Sea Animal**
15.	Crabs	**Sea Animal**

Arrange the planets from the 1st closest to the moon to the most distant.

1. **Mercury**
2. **Venus**
3. **Earth**
4. **Mars**
5. **Jupiter**
6. **Saturn**
7. **Uranus**
8. **Neptune**

Identify if the object is a solid, liquid or gas.

1. Desk — **Solid**
2. Milk — **Liquid**
3. Floor — **Solid**
4. Block — **Solid**
5. Air — **Gas**
6. Oxygen — **Gas**
7. Coffee — **Liquid**
8. Tea — **Liquid**
9. Carbon Dioxide — **Gas**
10. Wood — **Solid**
11. Tree — **Solid**
12. Soda — **Liquid**
13. Chair — **Solid**
14. Table — **Solid**
15. Hydrogen — **Gas**